CW00683947

Published by
Dark Windows Press
72 Llandudno Road
Rhos-on-Sea
LL28 4EJ
UK

www.darkwindows.co.uk
info@darkwindows.co.uk

The right of Desmond Morris to be identified as author
of this work has been asserted by him in accordance
with the Copyright, Designs and Patents Act 1988.

First Edition 2014

Printed in the UK

This edition published in 2014 in a limited
edition of 200 signed and numbered books.

ISBN-13: 978-1-909769-04-5

HEADWORKS

HEADWORKS

Collected poems, 1945 to 2014

Accompanied by a suite of paintings from the final quarter of 2013

DESMOND MORRIS

This is numbered copy 119 /200

Dark Windows Press
2014

PREFACE

In October 2013 I began a long series of small paintings based on a simple head-and-shoulders shape. In each one I experimented with irrational modifications of this basic form and I called these pictures my Headworks. In total there were 131 of them and I have selected 80 of these to accompany the texts in this book. They are shown in the order in which they were produced and details are given at the end of the book.

These paintings do not bear any specific relationship to the texts opposite them. They are provided to create a visual atmosphere of biomorphic imagery while the texts are being read. Although these pictures were all created in a burst of activity in the final quarter of 2013, beginning on October 3rd and ending on December 31st, the texts cover a much longer, 70-year period.

During the 70 years that I have been producing paintings I have completed over 2500 works, but have composed only 80 poems. They are rare because visual imagery has always dominated my thinking when I have been preoccupied with creating surrealist works. Words have been another part of my life altogether.

Although these surrealist writings have been referred to in the past as 'poems,' I prefer to think of them merely as jottings - odd notes dashed off when visual imagery did not satisfy me and I had to use a verbal form of expression instead to capture the perverse ideas that were rolling around inside my head.

Desmond Morris

Oxford, January 2014.

1

A TOAD

The sky mourned
a star that was killed
on the night that you were forced
from the weed of the tin-can pond.

As the star screamed,
your clumsy form began
and, finding no sympathy
among the weeds,
was sad.

You clung, a savage lover,
to your wrinkled pride,
no life more secret
and no secret better kept than yours,
a power as sorrowful as kind.

A star died to give the world a toad.

1945

THE ONE-EARED GODS

The one-eared gods of inopportune belly-laughs,

accentuated by one whimpers-worth

of visceral-warped female pebbles,

beleaguered by ornate inkpots

of a bygone era,

prostituted by the sisters

of the government's flag-sellers,

decided to reserve their occupation as essential,

owing to the national situation brought about

by the invention of synthetic women.

September 1947

THE GREAT WINGS

The great wings

of the poison penumbra

beat slowly above the heads

of the semi-intimate

as they small-talk their way home,

not a contraceptive's throw

from that breeding place of lonely houses

where pink crinkle and ivy rubber

are stowed in every love cupboard.

1947

THE LINCOLN WALLS

The Lincoln walls
and the hard green seduction
of the night's unwilling charge,
changing with the race of horses
and the race of blood,
to yet another yesterday.

And the sun had to shine.

March 1948

FOR LEONOR FINI

Her brush is a muted trumpet

and from her eyes

come bullets

that fail to penetrate

but splatter perfumed acid

on the surface of our tanks

and melt our snouting guns.

Her thoughts are metal feathers

that catch the wind

and quickly prod aside tomorrow's curtains,

showing some other place,

where seasons hold their fire,

an easy target for her loaded eyes.

November 1948

THE WELL-PLACED BALL

The well-placed ball
tears out the breast
pulled from the body's most illustrious folds
by unborn mutants
weaned on tube-struck foam.

It pits the throat with orange fins
until the shutting hinges
pinch the curving fear of stale distractions
that stain the underclothes of sterile hairs
until the cry is heard of swarming
pattern tales.

November 1948

THE GLEAMING LIMBS

The gleaming limbs ascend the virginal hills
of calm solidity,
watched by a year of salted yesterdays,
upon another's back,
waving to the several crowds who run apart
to show the engine's clothes
to nearby altar-pans whose single rims
reveal tomorrow's learned symmetry.

November 1948

THE VELVET SHIRT

The velvet shirt unwraps,

revealing unkind telephones

whose lines depart

to see the grandchild's chest of drawers,

from which a quiet sneezing sings

to the Amercan toilet…

…while all around walk stairs

upon which no hands may climb

to see the sonnet thrash from doors

unlocked to these ten sailors who,

changing their dresses,

tie their pockets to a shining can,

by which a laughing gate can open all our eyes.

November 1948

THE KETTLE-HEADED BOYS

The puckered teeth of the brain
roam around the palace grounds
searching nowhere for the uttered thoughts
that little words are needing,
and the slope is filled with the yellow desks
upon whose lobes these gentle screams
are spoken to an audience
of kettle-headed boys
whose pastimes are unheard of.

November 1948

10

SHOULDER HIGH

If there is a loud bang in your fingertips
never permit your reflection
to look at you from shop windows.

If you are sitting in a room with no ceiling
try and remember what time it was
when you had your first nose-bleed,
or the occasion when you climbed over
the third side of the fence of screaming reciprocals,
and heard a bell ringing in the distance.

The grass in the bedroom is damp
and it is probably better to wear
horn-rimmed spectacles
than burn your tongue.

But the heat from the mirror
that was a funeral gift
has brought on the rain.

The drops are very large
and each is falling several feet away
from its neighbours,
so that it is just possible not to get wet.

In the distance three firemen
are carrying off a plastic surgeon
shoulder high.

1948

THE SIDEWAYS MEN

The orange flowers of the sideways men
swing from the fifty debts of the ancient bottles
that belonged to the dejected clearing
beyond the folding hills
over the fence across the crimson field
where in our youth we stripped the moon.

1948

TWO SPHERES

The legs and toes of unlisted lives
wave to the winged plants
of some other minute.

Below the spines of glass stems
the fur coats are unlocked.

Around the sun and moon
a sphere engraves its name.

The daughters of the outsides
are coming in on toad-wings feathers.

ABC and the rain is dead -
welcome to your two spheres at once.

1948

SMALL PLEASURES

The colour of houses

Electric sparks

The eyes of animals

Old magazines

Smashing cracked crockery

The start of heavy rain

Unrusted tools

Sea-birds riding on the waves

The smell of new paint

The creases of hanging linen

The colour of smoke

How large animals lie down

Sheets of white paper

1948

EXOTIC HEADS

Exotic heads and happy unicorns
trample the antlers of the polar saucers
in the husband's library.

The fiddle on the floor
is sitting in front of the fire
without noticing the flowers in the chimney
and outside the air is crowded with boulders.

Squares of hairs are singing in parallel
with no particular aim in view
and the suicides on the edge
of the interminable armchairs
are feeling bored.

1949

WOMAN IN THE MOON

The face of the woman in the moon
is watching a young girl
who is reading the directions on a sealed box:

'If there is a fireplace at the bottom of your garden
never blow your lover's nose.'

She throws the box angrily to the ground.
Turning her face, she watches three men
as they walk down the street and into a building.
She follows them.

Three tables are sitting at a bar
smoking their ashtrays.
They separate as she enters and stand up straight.
Three of the halves are the three men.
With each is a woman holding a moistened shirt.

One of the three men receives a message
and they tie the shirts between their legs.
They begin to dance back and forth
in different coloured lights from a stained-glass window,
by which a weeping tree can tell the time of night.

The girl is sick.
She leaves by a series of revolving doors.
The glass in the first door is cracked,
in the second it is broken,
and in the third it is frosted over.

There is no glass at all in the fourth door
and through it she can see the sloping street.
In the distance a lorry runs over a peacock
but the driver does not stop.
He is looking at the face of the woman in the moon.

March 1949

TODAY IS THE DAY

Today is the day the time meant
when it wound up the clock with feathers.

I am late already for an appointment
with my taxidermist.
He has promised to insert two gaily-coloured beads
in my eye sockets
to render me more authentic
as I swing prettily in my little wicker cage,
frightening the passers-by with an occasional
sharp CAW-CAW.

1940s

17

HEAD HIGH

Christen the carpet with silver leaves.

Anoint the walls with suitable tableaux.

Cover the patch on the stairs

that the cloudburst knew

with glistening polished manners.

Relax the tight mists of forlorn regard

and snip the dead roots from the blistered boards.

Then with head held high,

and house in order

set out to question some other answer,

if only one is forthcoming.

1940s

18

THE DEATH OF LOLO

She was found in moleskin
(inside out) underclothes.
A press photographer wetted his camera
at the shock of seeing how wrinkled
her neck was.
An editor was sick over his stills.
The public came across her
with the second piece of toast.
A barrister shot himself in the mouth.
Six of her films were re-issued
with new titles.
Her collection of paradise birds was bought
by an admirer in the Argentine
who ran a zoo.
Her children took their fathers to her grave,
but once there, did not know what to do.
The set was unfamiliar.

1940s

19

THE LONG DISEASE

Live on an island
but take your vaccine
a small dose of the long disease.

Go soak yourself up
with ice-ceam crowds
and blood-and-thunder babies.

Witness the illegitimate
dance of the long-nosed women
and wag the head.

Wander the roads and roam the fields
of the monster's tentacles,
smelling his wounds.

1940s

SOFT CAT CALYX

Soft cat calyx
under little moons
stirring
with no wind's blather
as each other's stars
sway in this far-fetched
string of knots.

A forest would work
and no leaves seem harder
in a book of black silk memory
unless the pollen in her eyes
is shed to sting the skin
of the waterfall that never listens
to a single cry.

1950

21

AFTER-THOUGHTS

A clumsy nodule never clearing
up or down or inside round
the smooth eclectic sound
of mud petals sleeping
in and out the slanting moment
whose curse is only taken home
to bring about a coarser hair
upon the great fat little mat
when no-one calls for help
in hell upstairs
where children never go
until they die from day to day
on spiral springs
of acid after-thoughts.

1950

THE CLOWN'S GOWN

The clown's gown is worn

in towns whose rims smoulder

and flood with tears each sexless bladder

on these stumbling beaches

by and by and buy the best is always going first

and if again minutiae

escape the eye

come back yesterday

and slash your beaming backs outside

the striated banner box

in which no coloured balls can bounce

a tune quite half as well as

razors in a blistered book.

1950

23

BOTANY LESSON

The petals are falling
from the Freudian flower
as the precarious parrot
calls to its ancestors
to launch the lifeboat
that the one-eyed needle god
dubs wicked.

The flowers are dying
on the platonic planet
and the parrot seed is alive
and kicking the gong
in the temple
of the polygamous priest.

The plant is wilting
in the fidgeting field
which is ploughed by the ants
who strangled the vicar
with bootlaces.

And now the field is dead.

1950

24

A SMALL DESPERATION

Finding a crimson stone
on the edge of the carpet
there was nowhere to go,
there was nothing to do
except dust the weeping ornaments.

But tears are the property
of the cracked glass
and should not be dried.
Their stream fertilizes the grass
which can be made of coloured metal
or twisted swords.

Only now and again
can the clarity of mislaid temper
wield the blacksmith's hammer,
and blow after icy blow
solve this filthy honesty.

July 1950

25

SICKNESS OF THE LEGS

Sickness of the legs can be cured
by a wonderfully reflecting transparent rope,
but the cords hanging from the trees
are never clean enough to swing from
by one's hips.

Blood running to the head can be diverted
into graduated bottles
and the humidity may be calculated
to reveal the hideous beauty
of the drop of sweat
that is about to appear.

July 1950

THE ENVOY

The cephalized tauric envoy,
interrupted in translocation
by an enigmatic asteroid,
forms an irradiated union
blessed by the nunnery slaughterhouse
in waltz-time
every week.

January 1951

THE SCENTED LINE

Beyond the scented line,
the corrosion of my seeing limbs
grows soft with unbelievable spray
which staggers from the foliage
at your leaning feet.

The lips of my heart grow weak
at the threshold of your great vision
and my hunting bones subside,
attendant on the flight
of the white arrows' swarm.

February 1952

28

SACRED MILK

Come down the ladder

into our embrace

and find the focus

frowned with painted cracks

upon the smoking glass,

blinked with crooked cymbals

lain in disarray

until, hoarse-calling, the clinging sabres,

blessed with copper-crumbled grace,

unfrenzied below the nostril's flair,

can splinter into blind fountains,

cursing, teasing, pleading,

with a dying garland

bathed in sacred milk.

Easter 1952

29

TIDAL MEMORY

This is the poem of the destruction of rubble,
the song of the birth of beetles,
or of the rich crying of book-ends.

In the dying moment with sweet blunted points
there is no calling out
and the air is filled with water.

Tumbling, fur-lined bones, crystal leaves,
and petal-scales,
drift in light mists around the floor-beds.

This is the time of the caged grasses
the hour of abstract ritual,
or the infinite flickering that circles
the dimly-lit cavities of the mind.

With a slower pace
the solemn peace of tidal memory
finds itself alone, surrounded
by stupid, cursing waves.

August 1952

30

THE EVENING'S HORSES

The evening's horses
run their race
towards the simple shapes
of shadowed yesterday.

The night-wind's plumage
feels its flutter
ending in the target's rim.

Then my echoes are mingled
with the salt of a stone's shallow tears
calling softly to my mate
to unfold the story of her white seduction.

1952

THE GREEN EYE

Past the green eye
to the open field of incurable screens
I am driven
and wander, browsing with reluctance.

There must be an easy corner somewhere else
and a slight push in the wrong direction
would lead to a multi-coloured circle
in which black letters spell out
next year's mistakes.

1952

32

THE FACE OF MY BRAIN

Your limbs are mountains
on the face of my brain.

You are walking along the tightrope
that stretches between the eyes I have for you.

Yet all I can hear is your eyelashes
burning inside my ears.

Amongst these trees a small pile
of folded sheets lies silent,
the unused sails of a sexual yacht.

There is a rug lying upon the sea
and our voyage is pursued by scissors
that cut off the buttons
of our gaping volcanoes
as the Persians were said to do.

1952

33

THE PERFUMED HEELS

The perfumed heels
of the high-hoofed stallions
of the god of unwelcome spaces
clatter along the wretched miles
with which our swollen beings
feel their five chains broken.

Their tousled manes,
flowing on the wasted airs,
in which I see red birds
with red fleas climbing
in their plumage,
rise to the shallow firmament
and now the race is lost,
the tragedy bespoken,
the game a useless token.

1952

34

YOUR LARGE EYES

Why should your large eyes curse me
with your large stare?
By what strange laws
does your image never disappear?
Why should I care?

If the orange space
beyond your eyes,
beneath your brain,
will turn to tomorrow's bed,
I shall find myself asleep
and the clocks will tick away
until the grains of sand are painted blue.

Why are you calling me softly
when I am here
and why have your eyes become invisible?
What is the colour of your voice
that touches my throat
and quivers down my thoughts?

The swords hang crossed in sacrilege
on the walls of your being,
or lie shattered on the endless carpet.

1952

35

MALE WARNING

Do not jump on the ice,
it may break.

Do not hang from the branch,
it may break.

Do not raise your voice,
it may break
and then you will be a man
and they will expect you to
jump on the ice,
hang from the branch
and, if you are lucky, die clean.

If you are not, you will break,
and they will say 'aaaah'
and love you for the rest of your days.

1950s

OUT OF LIVING

I love you rude
I love you wicked
I cut you soft
I love you crude
I smell you rosy
I crush you cosy
I kiss you limp
I tell you noisy
I hate my loving
that is so bluntly
can you split
my prickly hide
can you spit
into my stumbling
see the source
where love is nursed
and twist it gently
until one moonday
I love you clean
from out of living.

November 1960

DAWN CHORUS

There are flowers on the grave of night

as day's embryo-hour

greets with hard pellucid stare

the haze of that nocturnal funeral

that has held

in its all-embracing void

the quiescence of a tomb

of royalty.

1960

STOP THEM IF YOU CAN

The end
stands at the corner of the field.

There is a follower whose rose's cobwebs
drip and spray the pollen of his tears,
until the undulating furrow
flows with arrows.

A flight of shafts moves
towards the orchard's wall
and to the prone beginning.

1960

NEVER LEAP

Never never
leap when
you can
crawl away.

My party's
over and
done with
great care
how you go
going going
gone…

January 1964

SHE IS

She is a rock pool

She is a field of blue poppies

She is a sneeze in the dark

She is a coloured lantern

She is an ice-cream in the desert

She is a dreaming hammock

She is a golden bottle whose label reads 'Now'

She is the ticker-tape

She is the Milky Way,

She is my burning snow, my avalanche of fire,

My stick of rock, my secret sand-dune,

My pendulum of timeless hours.

August 1964

41

TELL THEM WHERE TO GO

Do not cast a backward shadow,

there is nothing there,

a plastic flower, a clever twitch or two.

Do not listen to them,

you know their game, their sadness.

Take no notice.

They hate, and they adjust our clothing

before leaving, so no-one will ever know.

One shaven hair of yours

is worth six centuries of their teaching.

Tell them where to go.

July 1965

ANY BODY

Any body
will split the difference
and suck
the poison of a
lightning fork
spreadeagled
on the field of love.

1966

FLOWER POWER

We exhibit most in plants
those parts which
in ourselves
we try hardest to conceal.

Our unsightly sexual parts are private,
hidden away between our legs,
piously covered in opaque cloth.

The beautiful sexual parts of plants
- their wantonly coloured flowers -
are always public
and heavy with pollen.
We castrate them
to fill our vases.

1968

44

ANALYSIS

So I said to this analyst:
How much will you pay me per session?
He was outraged.
But how, I protested, can you value
what I say
if you do not have to pay for it?

That is my line, he roared.
You are out of your mind
I murmured softly.

Now see here, mother, he screamed,
pulling his plastic zip up and down.
But I am not your mother, I replied
with deadly calm.

Then why are you wearing
her after-shave lotion,
he hissed,
snapping his pin-pointed pencil
in three places.

May 1969

45

A SILENT GOODNIGHT

My feet are muslin-wrapped jelly

and the walls are turning a brighter red.

The room is lighter, then darker, sharper.

The music is richer, the food crisper,

My head rolls round in a perfect circle

Like a little metal ball.

I stumble in the snow, laughing.

At my hotel I demand to be taken to the 708th floor.

the lift-man stops politely

At the 7th and wishes me a silent goodnight.

January 1970

46

WIDE EYES

The slaughterhouses must be busy today.

Think of all the hungry people,

waiting for the butchers' shops to open,

eager to fondle the organs

of yesterday's wide-eyed calves and lambs,

arguing the price of someone's private kidneys.

The slaughterhouse will be even busier tomorrow.

March 1970

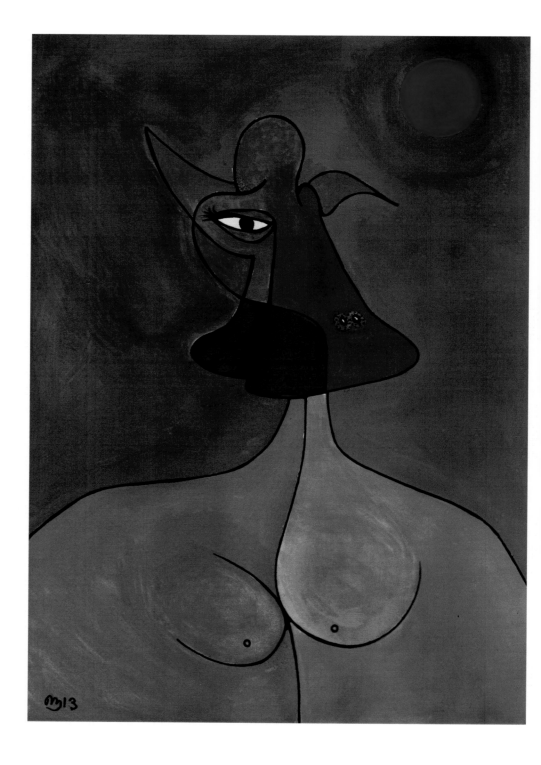

EVERY DRAWING

Every drawing rapes a page
with its first line.

Every painting deflowers a canvas
with its first stroke.

There must be an element of savagery
In that first creative moment

A more docile spirit would do well
to stick to gardening.

April 1970

THE BRAVE ART

It is much more difficult
to make a dishonest drawing
than it is
to write a dishonest sentence.

The artist is naked.
The author wears a mask.

Painters need more courage
than writers.

April 1970

LOVE IS A LIZARD

Love is a lizard,

handy with a fly,

hot on a flat

stomach stone,

quick of glance

and

slow in winter.

skin bright,

feather-tongued – clinging

like lichen,

vanishing

like

a

mirrored

smile…

April 1970

DARK INSIDE MY HEAD

There was a plop

in the well of my head

today.

An unseen hand

dropped something in.

Was it an accident?

Was it a jewel from a wrist,

or a pebble from a fist?

Or was it a small corpse,

the disposal of which

will foul the water of my thinking?

And how can I tell?

It is so dark inside my head.

1970

RIGHTS

we'll write

wheel wright

not right

knot rite

June 1970

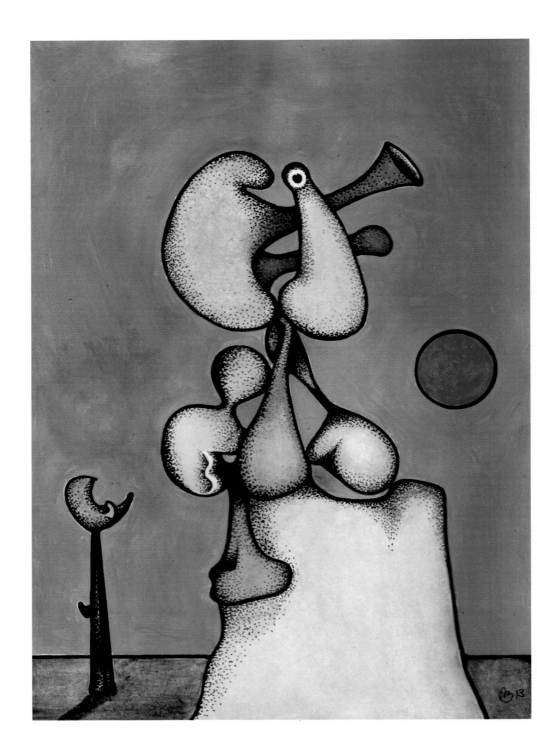

PRIZE FIGHT

The pen with the hooded nib
leapt from its corner
and mouthed terribly
at my large head.

Write me a bird of paradise,
it hissed,
or draw me the very last word
in forgotten script.

They tell me I am greater
than the sword
and that my ink is law,
so do as I say,
or stitch your lips together
for a hundred years.

1971

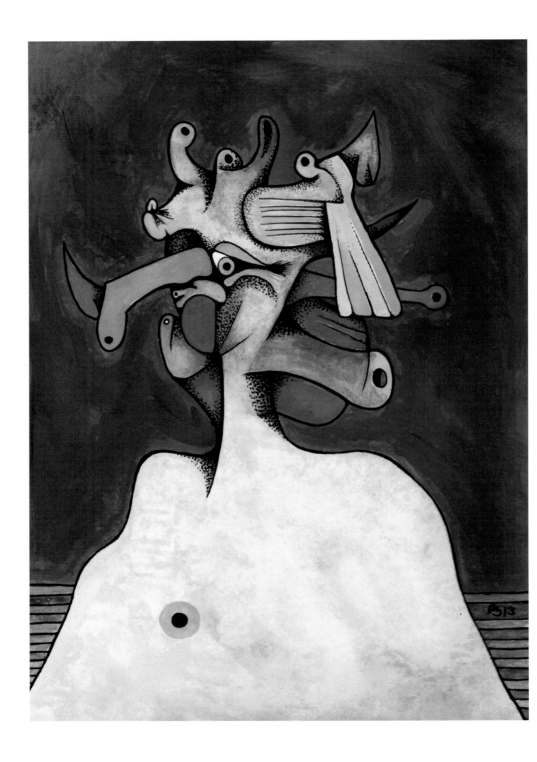

53

DARWIN OR LOSE

The Lesser or Romantic Mythopotamus
who became extinct last Friday
without much fuss
could trace his line
back a thousand million years
to a comely blob
called Jessica
whose single cell
was admired for its gently
curving walls.

He had come a long way
but in the end
his nostrils were his sad undoing,
so generous
that they attracted nesting birds
and left him short of breath
when feeding on green
emotions.

1971

FIRST AID

Thanks to the green film
that settles on top
of the rain-tub of life,
we advance today
like the hiker
who carries such a huge
first-aid kit
in his knapsack
that the weight of it
gives him blisters on his feet
for which he needs
first-aid.

1980

THE LOST ART

Leaves and hair-parcels
end their days in quiet
embrace with rising fears
and soft faces watching
the frosty glass.

Passing the long night
before the inner roots
start to nose their proud
beginnings, we are deaf to
the elephant's tidy song.

Smoke slides flat
in friendly waves
under the rim of the great bowl
that used to catch our tears
before we lost the art
of angry clowning.

April 1989

56

THE SOCKET OF GREEN

The socket of green,

close by the crowded limb,

calls to our moist palms

and dares our knotted tongue

to recall the day the clock stopped

with deep regrets that all our pains

are folded down

and stuck fast in the memory

of neglected eggs,

lying snug in the nest

of our longing.

1989

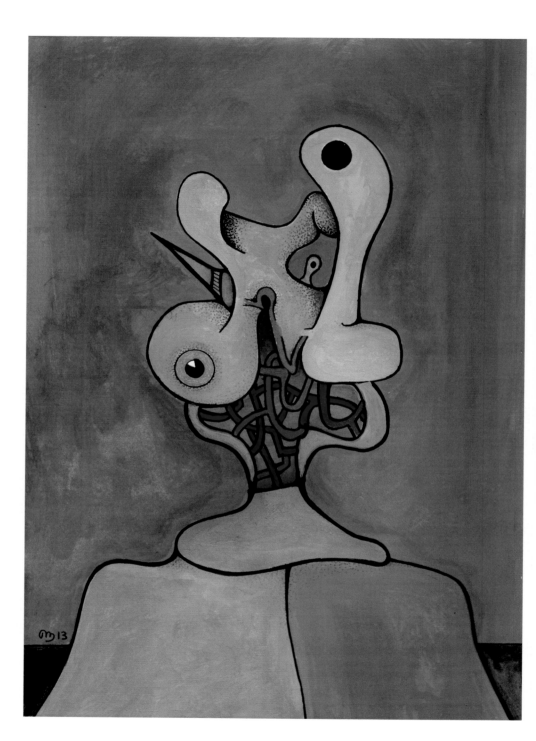

57

THE WHITE SHADOW

The white shadow of your absent form
blinds my brain with its bleak promises.

The smooth skin of your lazy neck
slides on my thoughts in slow caress.

The soft web of your laughing hair
strokes the eyes of my dark arrival
and all at once the room is empty.

Lost in caring, wondering why the siren is sounding,
the bells ringing, the lights flashing,
and the noise of dirty living
beyond these heavy walls
is so oppressive
and so foreign to my dreams.

October 1989

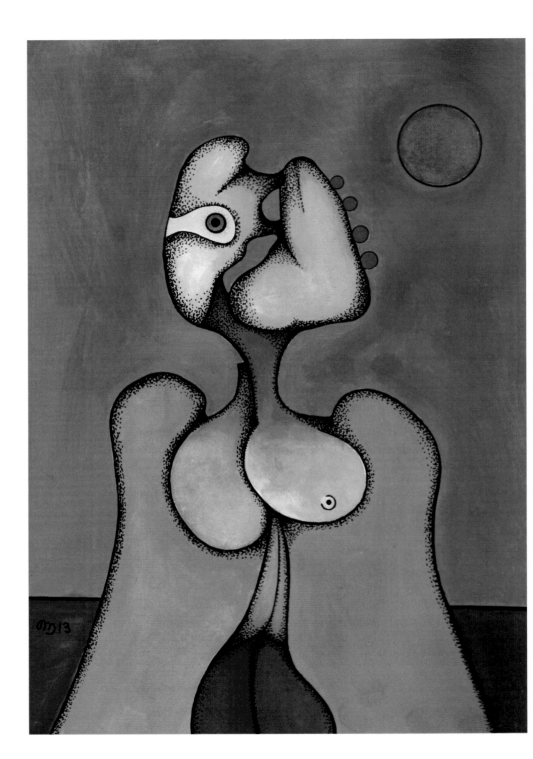

58

THE EDGE OF THE WORLD

The edge of the world was frayed
and slightly damp
where two firemen had coupled
in silent prayer.

Mosquitoes sucked at the table-cloth
as the diners ate their words
and bees made honey from the pollen
that hung between the thighs
of the distinguished guests,
ladies and gentlemen…

The edge of the world started to curl,
and disturb the metronome
of the bearded babies
that the showmen offered
to all and sundry.

Officials with far and narrow minds
came from near and wide
to dip their bread in the open wounds
of the Monday joint
and marvel at the resilience
of artificial limbs…

April 1990

59

THE OBSCENE SKY

As the obscene sky darkened,
the plumage of the dying sparrow
turned to hair
and its beak became teeth
through which it said in a deep voice:

I live in palaces where no eagle
dares to nest,
I drink in the gardens of the famous,
where no sad rarity will settle,
yet I am pest and they are paragon,
funded by fat egos with charity to burn.

Must I fail before they see me and
squeeze their watery eyes to find a tear
for my kind?

My droppings on them.

1990

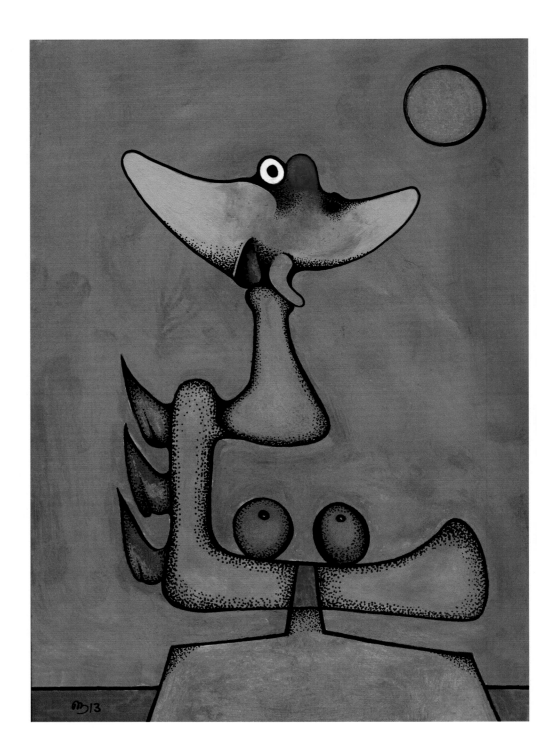

STARFISH

Starfish of the Silver Scream,
armed to hunt the wary glance,
fierce to see the easy killing,
sad to call the end of play.

Starwish for luck
in pain of parting.

1996

BODY BLOWS

If sleeping bodies lie,
then who can tell the truth
of the matter of fact
or fiction, said the girl
with the pierced nose
for a good story-teller.

If waking bodies mourn
then who will bury the eggs
in the garden of delights
that awaits me, said the girl
with something left to lose.

1996

THE OPEN BOOK

The golden apes of compromise

laughing at yesterday's fire

with endless sideways cries

climb into our open books

and give us feud

for thought in

the soft beds

of cosy night.

1996

KEEP LOW

Sleep up the night

sleep in the ice

sleep on the mound

rest under stone

crouch on the arm

sprawl on the rim

sleep at the core.

1996

COLA ROASTER

Customs
belong to
other shores tonight.

Our hands are lean
and hungry as we take
the ride to smell
the guns of life.

Our diet of
knives is
blunted by the echoes
of our daily fears.

We fly our flags
in the face of hidden
gestures…

1996

MORNING COMES

The dead song of public birds
heard today in private places
haunts the heads
of yellow flowers
whose task is uncertain.

The dead weight
of oval feathers
lining the hearts of those
who pay the price
of wide-eyed sleep,
clings to the limbs
of newborn fears
that call the tune
as morning comes.

1996

66

LAZY DAYS

Severed heads smile more
broadly when they are dry.

Long in tooth they glint
like vacant faces of the blind.

Their silent thoughts
melt like butter
in the mouths of caves
whose tunnels are almost endless.

Our foolish games
make tracks
in the bewildered
snow
as we leave the
scene
to die another day.

1996

YESTERNIGHT

Last day

I saw

a red

form

moving through

the repulsive vegetation that lies

around the valves that

open the mouths of

our dead

conundrums…

1996

OUR SAD PARADE

Pain plays its own tune
sweet and high inside
the folds of family skin.

Watching the dry waves
of polite fear that sucks the air
between the toes of strangers,
there is no escape
from the knowing stares
of the increasingly bland
ladies and gentlemen
who slowly cheer our sad parade.

1996

LOSING PLACE

Losing place on pain of life
is of itself a fine
defeat.

Holding skin in gaping line
is only losing
space.

Holding breath is never seen
in dancing
limbs unless
the trickle of
salt is licked
in moonlight.

1996

BAD DAY

On a sunny night in Belgium
the navel frocks are tawny red
with sweet concern.

This is not a pipe-dream
hissed my gritty friend,
casting his line over my eye.

Bad day, suck tight.

July 1997

ONLY THE BIRDS

Only the birds

can hear the light

smell the songs

taste the rhythm of the days

and wish the leaves of time

would fall.

November 1997

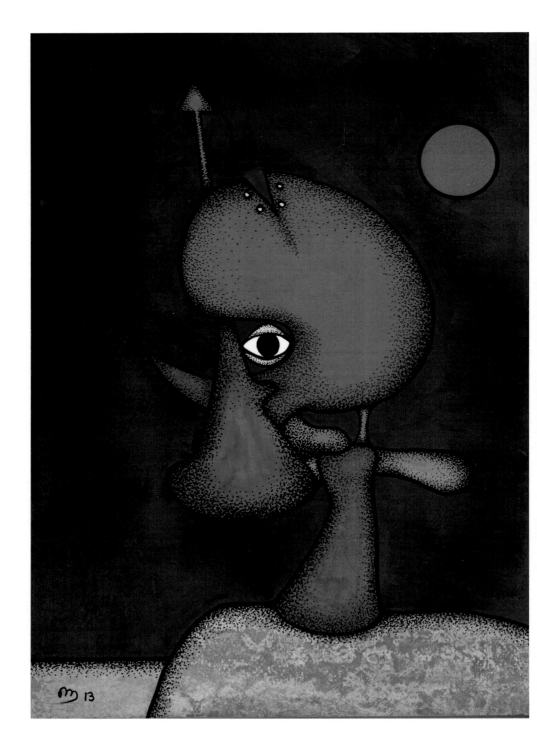

THE AIR

The air is thin
as the mountains climb down
their slopes to lick their
valleys clean of pain.

The air is thick
with words of protest
and tiny lies in beds of rice
planted by parallel bars.

The air is cool
with cubes of lice
singing the charms
of passing
bishops.

Amen.

April 1999

TWICE UPON A TIME

Twice upon a time
sharing our saucers
flying to our dreams
of hidden pleasures
we lie to one
another's arms.

We whisper between our
legs and tell each
other's tales of red
tape and rape in the
hushed tones of mock
surprise.

Every day.

November 2000

DEAD FACES

Dead faces always grin in the end
as lips retreat from the hushed
tones of spiteful praise heaped
on their heads as hot necks
crane their way into
the pits of the arms dealers
in their expensive black suits.

A gun is not a gun today, say the
graffiti sprayed by eyeless twins.

November 2000

75

IN YOUR MOUTH

Sunrise butterflies
soar to your open lips.

Morning butterknife
slices your lazy thoughts.

Midday butterdish
melts in the songlight.

Afternoon butterfingers
suck on your artful tongue.

Evening buttercups
feel your sad secret my
midnight butterscotch.

December 2001

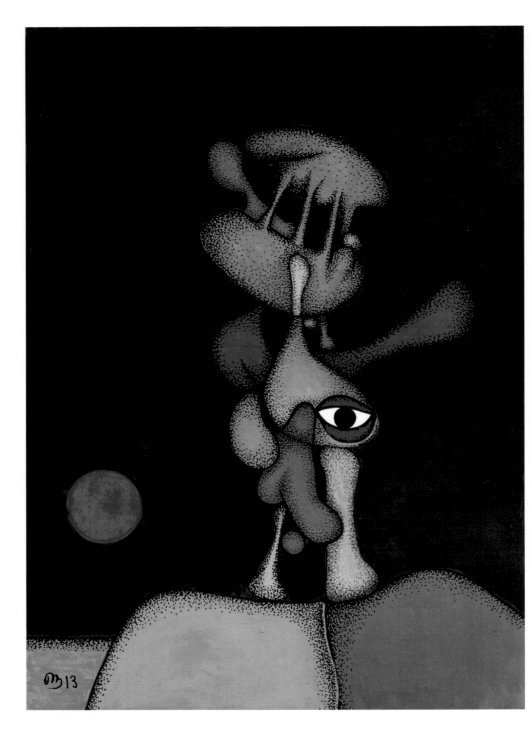

A FORT NIGHT

A fort night at the night fort
costs as little as a broken foot
for those who sing like echoes
in the morning sky

December 2004

THE SMALL BANG

Oh my ME! said God,
when arrested
for crimes against humanity.
Just because I went bang
all those years ago
don't imagine
I give a dying duck
about the mould
on a rotting planet.

Just my luck said Gabriel,
there he goes again,
giving the Almighties
a bad name.
Wait until God's God
hears about this.
He'll be as mad as heaven.

Who said
Dark Matter
doesn't matter?

August 2012

78

THE INSPECTION

The inspectors are coming
with their soft-boiled smiles
and their convex folders
to examine our navels,
inserting their probes into our dreams,
extracting the soft centre of our shells
and blending it with molten numbers
to arrive at the answer they already knew.
Please go away; like sad Garbo
we want to be alone.

December 2013

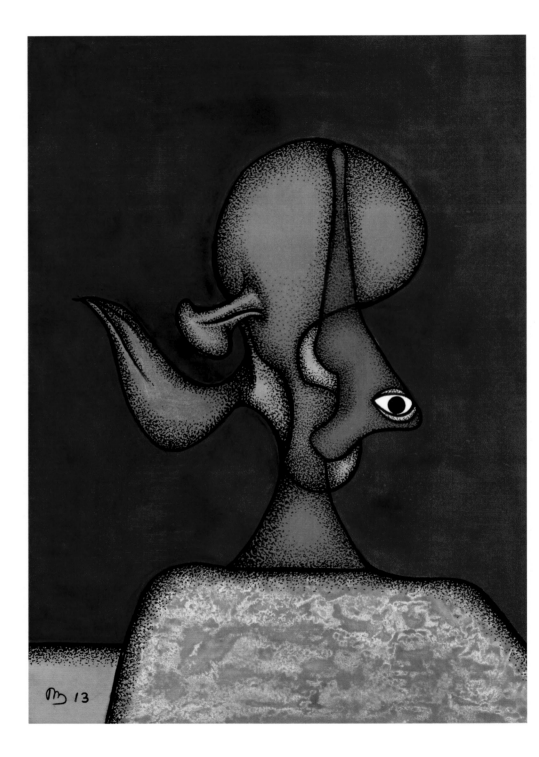

79

GLOWWORMS

It is so dark inside my head
that I must search the hillside for glowworms
who are falling in love
and insert them gently into my ears
so that I can hear their light.

With their help I must explore
my most private thoughts,
hidden in bundles of dreams,
before they are shredded
by my oppressive logic.

December 2013

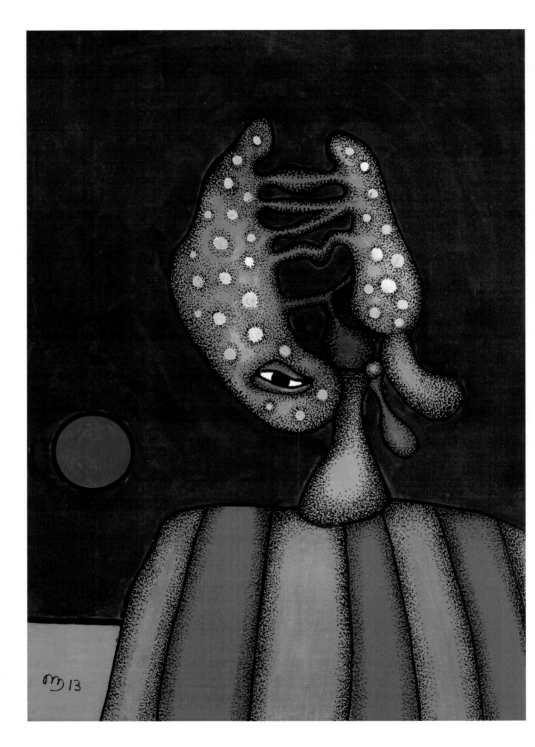

80

THE CAGE OF LOVE

Inside each well-versed face

behind the mask whose name

we no longer know

there lies an open wound

that spells the time of night

when we are quite alone

and climbing plants attach

their curious tendrils

to stop out flight

from the truth

we will not share

until we die and

cease to struggle

inside the cage of love.

January 2014

THE PAINTINGS

Of the 80 paintings shown, the first 40 are monotypes – oil line drawings with added watercolour. The second 40 are ink drawings with added watercolour. They have been chosen from a suite of 131 paintings (all A4 size: 29.7 x 21 cm.) completed in October, November and December 2013. The titles have been chosen almost arbitrarily, to provide labels for the individual works. The details are as follows:

1.   2013/19 FIGURE IN THE NIGHT. (3rd October)

2.   2013/21 THE FAVOURED ONE. (5th October)

3.   2013/22 FORGOTTEN FIGURE. (6th October)

4.   2013/24 THE FATALIST. (8th October)

5.   2013/25 THE FAITHFUL ONE. (9th October)

6.   2013/26 THE FORGIVER. (9th October)

7.   2013/27 FIRM FIGURE. (9th October)

8.   2013/29 FASHIONABLE ONE (9th October)

9.   2013/30 THE FANATIC (10th October)

10.   2013/34 FLUSTERED FIGURE (11th October)

11.   2013/36 FORMIDABLE FIGURE (11th October)

12.   2013/37 THE FEARMONGER (11th October)

13.   2013/38 THE FREETHINKER (11th October)

14.   2013/39 THE FACTFINDER (12th October)

15.   2013/40 THE FAINT-HEARTED (12th October)

16.   2013/41 THE FIXER   (12th October)

17.   2013/42 FRETFUL FIGURE (12th October)

18.   2013/43 THE FORWARD-THINKER (12th October)

19.   2013/44 FRUSTRATED FIGURE (12th October)

20.   2013/45 FOOLHARDY FIGURE (13th October)

21.   2013/48 THE FORBEAR (13th October)

22.   2013/49 THE FLUENT FRIEND (13th October)